D1121520

WATCHING ANIMALS IN NATURE

BY ABBY COLICH

BLUE OWL
BOOKS

TIPS FOR CAREGIVERS

Social and emotional learning (SEL) helps children manage emotions, learn how to feel empathy, create and achieve goals, and make good decisions. One goal of teaching SEL skills is to help children care for themselves, others, and the world around them. The more time children spend in nature and the more they learn about it, the more likely they will be to appreciate it and receive its emotional benefits.

BEFORE READING

Talk to the reader about the concept of observing animals in their natural habitats.

Discuss: What kinds of animals do you see when you go outside? What are animals doing when you see them outside? What is your favorite animal that you see when you spend time in nature?

AFTER READING

Talk to the reader about how watching animals makes him or her feel. Discuss the benefits of feeling connected to nature.

Discuss: How do you feel after spending time outside watching animals? What are some ways you can watch animals if you cannot go outside? Why is it important to respect animals and their homes in nature?

SEL GOAL

Children may struggle with processing their emotions, and they may lack accessible tools to help them do so. Explain to children that nature can help people feel good. Watching animals can help children feel calmer, learn compassion, and have respect for nature. Encourage children to find a way to feel more connected to animals. Whether they are watching birds, looking for bugs, or listening to a recording of animal sounds, nature offers many ways to connect with animals.

TABLE OF CONTENTS

CHAPTER 1

ANIMALS EVERYWHERE

Animals live on every part of Earth. Some fly in the sky. Others hide underground. Others run, swim, or hop.

Where do you see animals? No matter what animals you see or where you see them, watching them can help you **focus** your attention. It can help you feel more connected to the world around you.

You can practice **mindfulness** while watching animals. How? Put your worries aside. Focus on the present.

Be quiet and still. Waiting to see an animal can help you learn **patience** and **self-control**. You don't want to scare it away.

CHAPTER 2

HOW TO WATCH

Research what animals you might see nearby. Plan ahead and know where you want to go to watch them. Some animals **migrate** or **hibernate** when the seasons change. The animals you see might depend on the time of year.

binoculars

Go with an adult or have an adult's permission to be outside. Check the weather before you go. Make sure you are dressed for it. Decide if you need equipment like binoculars or a magnifying glass.

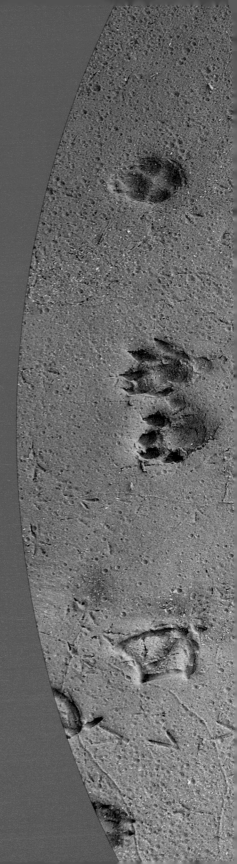

When you get there, set up a comfortable spot. Put away your **devices**. Focus on what you see, hear, smell, and feel. You might not see **wildlife** right away. But you can look for signs that animals were there. Tracks, nests, poop, shells, or shed skin are all signs an animal has been near.

LOOK, DON'T TOUCH!

Observe how animals act when you enter their **habitats**. Do they seem frightened or **stressed**? Keep quiet. Try not to make sudden movements. Don't touch or try to feed a wild animal. Never touch or move an animal's home, eggs, or babies. You could get hurt or make the animal sick.

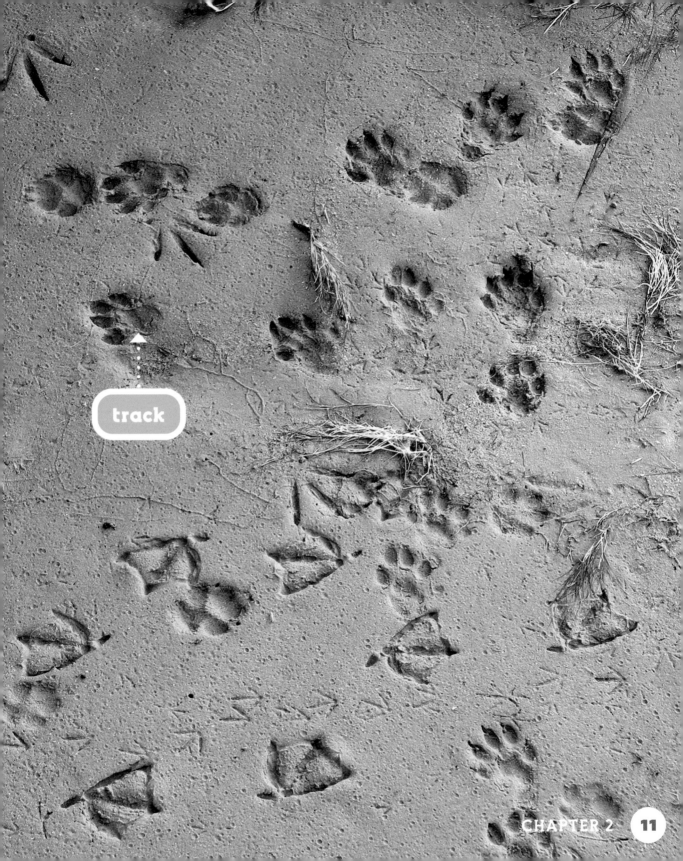

track

CHAPTER 3

WAYS TO WATCH ANIMALS

What animals can you see? What are they doing? Notice how they **behave**. How do they move? What noises do they make?

Walk the same route in your neighborhood a few days in a row. Do you see the same animals each day? Are they doing anything differently? Maybe a squirrel is collecting nuts in the fall. Why? It is preparing for winter!

You can watch birds from almost anywhere. First, close your eyes and listen for them. Then, open your eyes and look. Binoculars can help you see birds that are far away. If you don't have any, that is OK. Follow a bird with your eyes as it flies, swims, or moves on land.

LIKE A BIRD

Close your eyes. Imagine you are flying like a bird. How does the air feel on your face? What can you see from up high?

Insects are all around during warm times of the year. Look for slugs or worms that squirm by. Wait for a bee or butterfly to land on a flower. Or watch a spider spin its web.

Look closely. Use a magnifying glass if you have one. Do you see eyes or a pattern on its body?

RESEARCH ANIMALS

Have you ever seen an animal but didn't know what it was? With an adult's help, use an app or guidebook to help you **identify** animals.

magnifying glass

If you can't go outside, try looking out a window. How many animals can you see from inside? You can watch animals at a zoo, farm, or aquarium.

Just looking at photos or watching videos of animals can also help you feel more relaxed. An adult can help you find animal videos online.

Watching animals will help you respect them. You can work to keep their habitats safe. Pick up litter in your neighborhood. Or raise money to help animals that are **endangered**. What are other ways you can help animals?

GOALS AND TOOLS

GROW WITH GOALS

Watching animals can help you feel relaxed and more connected to nature.

Goal: Research your favorite animal. What is one fact you learned that surprised you?

Goal: Keep an "animals in nature" journal. Write about or draw pictures of the animals you see. Do this at least once a week. Pay attention to the animals you see and how they change throughout the year.

Goal: Imagine you are a fish in the ocean or a tiny bug on a giant tree. How does the world look to you?

MINDFULNESS EXERCISE

Find a recording of birds chirping, frogs croaking, or another animal sound that you find relaxing. Find a comfortable place to sit. Put down your device and close your eyes. Sit up straight and stay still as you listen. Slowly breathe in and out. Do this for a few minutes. How do you feel when you finish? Are you more relaxed and focused?

GLOSSARY

behave
To act in a particular way.

devices
Pieces of equipment with computers inside, such as smartphones or tablets.

endangered
In danger of becoming extinct.

focus
To concentrate on something.

habitats
Places where certain animals or plants normally live.

hibernate
To sleep or rest through the winter.

identify
To recognize or tell what something or who someone is.

migrate
To move from one area to another at different times of the year.

mindfulness
A mentality achieved by focusing on the present moment and calmly recognizing and accepting your feelings, thoughts, and sensations.

observe
To watch someone or something closely, especially to learn something.

patience
The ability to put up with problems or delays without getting angry or upset.

research
To collect information about something.

self-control
The ability to restrain or control oneself, especially relating to one's feelings and actions.

stressed
Experiencing mental or emotional strain.

wildlife
Living things, especially animals, that live in their natural habitats.

TO LEARN MORE

FACT SURFER

Finding more information is as easy as 1, 2, 3.

1. Go to www.factsurfer.com
2. Enter "**watchinganimalsinnature**" into the search box.
3. Choose your book to see a list of websites.

INDEX

Blue Owl Books are published by Jump!, 5357 Penn Avenue South, Minneapolis, MN 55419, www.jumplibrary.com

Library of Congress Cataloging-in-Publication Data
Names: Colich, Abby, author.
Title: Watching animals in nature / by Abby Colich.
Description: Minneapolis, MN: Jump!, Inc., 2021.
Series: Nature heals | Includes index. | Audience: Ages 7–10
Identifiers: LCCN 2020034237 (print)
LCCN 2020034238 (ebook)
ISBN 9781645278467 (hardcover)
ISBN 9781645278474 (paperback)
ISBN 9781645278481 (ebook)
Subjects: LCSH: Nature–Psychological aspects–Juvenile literature. | Animals–Juvenile literature.
Nature, Healing power of–Juvenile literature. | Mindfulness (Psychology)–Juvenile literature.
Classification: LCC BF353.5.N37 C648 2021 (print) | LCC BF353.5.N37 (ebook) | DDC 155.4/1891–dc23
LC record available at https://lccn.loc.gov/2020034237
LC ebook record available at https://lccn.loc.gov/2020034238

Editor: Eliza Leahy
Designer: Michelle Sonnek

Photo Credits: Shutterstock, cover, 1, 3, 4; CGN089/Shutterstock, 5; JohnnyGreig/iStock, 6–7; Africa Studio/Shutterstock, 8 (left); Steve Collender/Shutterstock; 8 (right); all_about_people/Shutterstock, 9, 16–17; Zoltan Major/Shutterstock, 10–11; Gabbie Berry/Shutterstock, 12; electricpark-photo/Shutterstock, 13; LightField Studios/Shutterstock, 14–15; wavebreakmedia/Shutterstock, 18–19; Dani Llao Calvet/Shutterstock, 20–21.

Printed in the United States of America at Corporate Graphics in North Mankato, Minnesota.